SAY IT LIKE A MEXICAN

Robert Challen de Mercer

Robert Challen de Mercer © Copyright 2006

All rights reserved

No parts of this publication may be reproduced,
stored in a retrieval system, or transmitted in any
form or by any means, electronic, mechanical,
photocopying, recording or otherwise without the
prior permission of the copyright owner.

British Library Cataloguing In Publication Data
A Record of this Publication is available
from the British Library

ISBN 1846854326
978-1-84685-432-3

First Published 2006 by

Exposure Publishing, an imprint of Diggory Press,
Three Rivers, Minions, Liskeard,
Cornwall, PL14 5LE, UK
WWW.DIGGORYPRESS.COM

PRINTED ON ACID FREE PAPER

Also by the author:-

"Sip of a Complex Broth"
Insights from Baja and Mainland Mexico.

"Charged Particles"
Poetry Anthology.

Table of Contents

Greetings: Saying Hello and Goodbye	17
Saying Yes, No, and Nothing	18
You and Me	19
Being Cool or Plain Ugly	19
Adding Emphasis	20
Showing Approbation or Revulsion	21
Lounge Lizards	21
Being a Fuckor or a Fuckee	22
Getting Turned On	22
Take it Easy, Man!	23
What a Bummer!	23
Some Everyday Slang	23
Lighten Up, Bro'!	25
What a Bloody Creep!	25
Some English Terms in Mexican Spanish (A Foxy Chick: A Cute Dude (Bloke!)	27
The Money Honey	28
Whores, Cuckolds and "Cabrones"	29
The World's a Gas!	30
Moctezuma's Revenge	31
More on Finance	31
Sweat of the Brow and Debts	32
Gimme a Break!	32
Sex, Drugs and Other Foibles	33
The Penis	33
Having a Ball with Slang	34
Leave it to Beaver	35
Bristols, er, Breasts	36
The Bottom Line	37
Making Love	38
The Hated Sheath	40
Self Relief	41

More on the World's Oldest Business	42
Homosexuals	43
More on Drugs	44
Tobacco, coke and heroin	
Old Bill (The Fuzz)	48
The Hoosegow (Jail)	49
Communicating with Family and Friends	51
The Kids, Lovers, Others	
More Everyday Words Borrowed by Slang	53
More on Being Cool	55
…And Uncool	
Simpatico : A Desired Characteristic	57
Humor is Alive and Well in Mexico	58
More on Being Attractive	59
Pesos: that Scarce Commodity	61
Using Money	62
Border Talk	63
Final Word; Inequality under Mexican Law	64

Introducing the Author

Robert Challen de Mercer has worked as a reporter, columnist and teacher for many years in Mexico and Spain. He has had a column in several English language publications, including the Mexico City News, the Union de Morelos and newspapers in Baja. He has also had articles published in leading North American magazines; contributed in producing specials for BBC TV and Discovery Channel. The author has also published a book on Mexico, "Sip of a Complex Broth" and an anthology of poetry, "Charged Particles."

Apart from writing, Robert has worked in many jobs in several countries, including the UK, Spain, Mexico, Australia and the USA. He is now semi-retired and lives in South Baja, Mexico and England.

Introduction to Mexican "Modismos."

Slang is devised to amuse, insult, convey double meanings and cement friendship among "homeys". The idiom is often raw and pithy and makes no apology for content. It pokes fun at sacred cows and many facets of the human condition. Slang has been the sword of the oppressed and the lingua franca of the poor, and poorly educated for centuries.

Every nation, to some degree, has invented its own linguistic sub-culture, which has spread throughout all the citizens. Street talk may insult, but it also enriches; it allows fun to be poked, usually without real harm; it is often very astute and poetic and it keeps us from false pride. More than anything else, it can be really entertaining to listen to or read.

As in English, or any other complex world language, Mexican Spanish carries many colloquial terms which are generally never understood by people from other nations. Even Spanish from the mother country has many "street" additions of its own, along with many of those shared with Mexico and other Hispanic countries.

Much slang is of a sexual nature, including oaths and insults and terms for forbidden substances; it needs to be well understood by those weak in Spanish before they practice the words with their Mexican hosts, otherwise they may only succeed in insulting when they merely intended to amuse.

Mexicans love verbal contests using double meanings; this writer, who speaks good Spanish, has been left red faced and gasping on the sidelines many times in attempting to beat Mexicans at their own game. They especially enjoy teasing their heterosexual friends by insinuating they have gay tendencies; they will also enjoy making the Gringo a target for this funning. Good advice is, take it with a smile, but don't get involved, you will never have the last word and may end up becoming the offended one, which will only amuse them more.

Apart from the mysterious slang, many words in Spanish have a different meaning from the one they sound like in English: "constipado," for example, has little to do with a gummed-up bowel, as it merely means to have a cold; "embarazado" might leave you embarrassed if you don't soon realize it means also to be pregnant; "simpatico" doesn't mean you are sympathetic, but rather you are empathetic and an all-round good guy: The list goes on.

Most slang in Mexico is born in the poor barrios of the inner city. The Capital or D.F. as it is commonly called, for Distrito Federal, is a hodgepodge of approaching 30 million people, depending on who's "damned lies" you read. The government statisticians are persuaded to paint a far healthier picture than is really the case. Their guestimates of 16 million or so are laughable to the man on the street. In any event, life to an observer from the First World is truly horrendous in poor colonias (suburbs) such as Tepito, for example. The colorful idiom born in these crucibles helps make life bearable for those with no escape.

It is this rich idiomatic sub-culture that is the subject of this modest book; a useful tool to anyone visiting or intending to spend some time in this wonderful country of Mexico. Much of slang included also applies to most Spanish-speaking countries.

Let's be clear about the content…

If you are the type of person who is easily offended by images conjured-up by the written word, perhaps this book is not for you.

Slang, by its very nature, is often used to accurately portray the human condition: our foibles, habits, physiology, sexuality, ugliness, (as perceived), weaknesses, and official capacity - along with all the demons that are contained in the Pandora's Box of human character.

As such, modismos capture no prisoners: they are often hilarious, pithy, succinct, sarcastic or downright rude and offensive; they can make you laugh or gasp. But one thing is for sure, without some knowledge of the language invented by Mexican street people –much of which is in everyday usage by one and all - you will never be a fluent Spanish speaker, or be truly accepted by your hosts.

Finally, please remember, if you are upset by any of the slang terms featured within, don't kill the messenger!!

N.B. As the reader studies this book, he will notice some repetition of the slang words and expressions used. The author has left these in place to help clarify what is a complex and ever-changing form of communication, often vague in its use..

Pronunciation

After floundering dreadfully, I have decided not to try to include phonetic advice on pronunciation after each word, phrase, or sentence in Spanish. There was just too much volume and attempting this left the text looking like some obscure hieroglyphics. Just remember Spanish speakers pronounce all the vowels and consonants (with few exceptions), so keep you ears open to improve your pronunciation. I have also left out accent marks above letters, because they won't help you pronounce words unless you are close to being bilingual, but rather confuse the issue further. (The "Ñ" excepted as it changes the "n" into a "ny" sound).

One important thing to understand is that Spanish speakers don't mumble, although they usually speak quietly. Leave the muttering and mumbling for the Anglo's whose language and mouth position lends itself to this. In Spanish, it is mandatory that you open and stretch your mouth and lips in order to pronounce all the letters. Say "Español," for example, (Eh-spahn-yohl): That's it! Move those lips!!

A brief guide to help the novice.

The ubiquitous "ñ" (say "enya"). (The "n" with the accent above) is very common and pronounced "ny" as in niño ("ninyo" male child)
Causing trouble is the double "ll" sound which becomes a hard "y" like in "llaves" ("yaves" keys).
"j" is said like an "h" ("hacaranda" jacaranda)
"h" is always silent ("hora"…ora, hour).
"v" and "b" are interchangeable as regards pronunciation. ("yerba bueno or yerva bueno"…the good herb).
"x" is often interchangeable with "j" As in the word "Mexico," some purists (read nuisances) say it should be "Mejico."

Most words are accented on the second to last syllable (unless other syllables carry accents) and words ending in "l" or "r" are emphasized on the last syllable.

Vowels.

A … soft and long, as in "caca" (cahcah, slang for poo-poo!)

E… becomes an "eh" sound, ("mete" mehteh to interfere)

I… becomes a double e "ee" sound ("mire" meereh, look)

O… A short sound, as in "hot" ("popo" another slang term for poo-poo! Also abbreviation for the volcano Popocatepetl)

U… Almost a double o "oo" sound as the English prude ("usted" oostehd, you).

Y… hardens and takes on a "dy" sound ("Yolanda" dyohlahndah).

Greetings: Saying Hello.

"Hello" can be said in several ways. It directly translates as "Hola" (ola)..."H" is silent in Spanish). But Mexicans often say "Cubo," especially to youngsters. "Que onda?" Roughly, "What's happening?" Traditionally, next would be "Como esta Usted," "How Are You?" This is often replaced by "Como estamos?" Or "How are we?" (All). You may hear "Buey," or "Ox," tacked on the end of greetings, it's like mate in British English, or perhaps "buddy," or homeboy in the USA. Very good friends also call each other "Cabron," Lit. "goat," but used as bastard here...stay away until you have lived here years!

"Que transas," the cool way to say "Que onda". Loosely, this would mean how are you manipulating your life as Transa is cheat.

"Goodbye" has just as many imitators. You all know "Adios" if not, don't bother trying to assimilate words herein, learn some basic Spanish first. Commonly, "Nos vamos." Lit. "We go," or "Let's hit the road." More formally you hear, "Hasta manana," "Until tomorrow," "Hasta luego" or simply "Luego," Which means "Then," or "Later" in this context.

More on the mysterious "Onda," a word once the property of the young, now in general usage everywhere.

An onda, literally, is a wave, (hence the "wave" that sweeps sports stadiums all over the world and began in Mexico's huge Azteca Stadium is the "Onda").

Apart from the literal use, Onda is not easy to translate. Perhaps the "Way something happened," comes close.

Apart from the common Que onda?" (above) you have "Asi es la onda Mexicana," "That's how we do it here."

"Le tiro la onda" "He flirted with her."
"Cual es tu onda?" What are your likes and dislikes - what do you do?
"Que bueno onda" "That's great!" Something nice was done by someone.

"Yes" and "No."

All the rage in Mexico City in the 90's, but now used less, were "Simon" for "Si," or yes. And "Nel pastel" for "No" (A friend of mine always said "Ni" for no (as "Si" is yes, but it didn't catch on). To emphasize the negative, "No," first say "Ya...no!" "Ya!" is a lovely two letter expletive used when "enough!" is needed to be said forcibly...just "Ya!" will stop a kid or pet in its tracks. Like our "Hey," or "Oi! but even more emphatic. You might hear many derivations of the above: the affirmative and negative with tails added for poetic effect. "Is varnish" and "Nones cantones" are two.

"Nada" "Nothing," is one of the better known Spanish words, thanks to writers such as Hemingway, who used it all the way through his atheistic version of the Lord's Prayer: "Nada that is in Nada. Nada be Thy Name,..." Etc. Along with Nada, you get the ubiquitous "No hay," which doesn't mean there is no cattle food, but simply "There isn't any." Period. This usually expressed with a shrug of resignation in this country where to run out of supplies of a given item is de rigueur. Along with No hay, comes "Ni Marta," "Not a Bit," and "Ni suenos," "not in your dreams, buster!" Finally, you may guess that "No hay nada," means there's nothing at all.

You and Me

The same poetic licence for Si and No is applied to the first and second person singular, Usted, (Tu, familiar) and I (Yo). You may hear, "Yolanda," "Melon," "Menta," even the English "Me," and others.

Being Cool or Ugly Invokes Mum and Dad

There's as many ways to indicate what is in or out in both English and Spanish, and they are added upon regularly. As we now have the awful "Minger." "Slapper" in the UK, along with the overused 'Wanker," nouns of approbation and condemnation appear in Spanish, lose favour and fade. The obviously sexist and traditional way to indicate the worth of anything is "Padre," father, for good things, or degree, and poor old "Madre," mother, for items of scorn. Therefore, "Me vale madre," means "I don't give a shit," whereas "Aye, que padre!" is "Oh, How super." While shooting the bird in Mexico, people will say, "Tu Madre," a contraction of "Chingar tu madre," the great insult over which many lives have been lost. "Madrear." To beat something into submission. Or "Te voy a romper la madre." "I'm going to knock the stuffing out of you!" Along with ""Un madrazo," anything with a kick to it - from an actual blow to a strong drink, etc. "Lo sacaron a madrazos." he was ejected violently. "Ni madres," either, "not on your nelly," or, "Yeah, I could cocoa."
Also:- "Hubo madrazos," There was a fight.
"A la madre," (or "Madres"). "Holy cow!"
"Estoy hasta la madre." I'm legless"...pissed as a parrot.

"Ese lugar esta haste la madre de gente." Place is bursting at the seams with people.

"Poca Madre." Very common usage. Depending on the rest of the sentence can be super or awful.

Examples. "Ese jugador es poca madre!" The player is phenomenal.

"Que poco madre que tu mujer salio con el jardinero." "What a bummer, your wife screwing the gardener!"

A good comeback for fielding "Madre" and other insults is "A viente!" Back at you. In response to "Chinga tu madre," the Mexican classic insult, "a viente," is useful because it usually restores the status quo without worsening the conflict and without the original speaker of the insult loosing face. (Also "A la tuya!" "Yours as well").

Adding Emphasis.

Adding "...isimo" to an adjective lends force to the intent. "Padrisimo," is the ultimate in super cool.

"Chido" is a hippy word loosing appeal. Means cool or rad.

Another very helpful word Mexicans use to express approval or disgust is "Barbero," or "Que barbero!" This is a nice word that rolls well off Anglo tongues. The "Que" in front of the word is to express disgust: "The Americans have bombed Irak"..."Que barbero!!" "Barbero," used alone can often mean something is rad or super cool (Like "Padre," remember?) Adding to the confusion is "Barbaridad," such as, "They went to bed on the first date," "Que barbaridad,"...("How disgusting"), or "Que padre," depending on your outlook on life. Lastly, you often hear "Se cuesta una barbaridad," "It was very expensive." Barbero, then, might be likened to the English "Awful, " also used to express disgust and approval. Another common pejorative is "Mendigo," it actually means beggar, but can be used for a person or object in a scathing way, "El es un mendigo" a jerk or a wanker.

Showing Approbation or Revulsion.

"Me cae bien." Caer is to fall, so this saying indicates the person has "fallen" into liking someone. Even, "Me cae enamorado," "I fell in love." On the other hand, "Me cae gordo" or "I have a fat dislike," says the opposite. Gordo meaning fat. Don't use the better known "Gusta" for people of the same sex or folks might suspect you are gay. Like "Me gusta ella" is OK man to girl, but "Me cae bien" for your male bud or strangers of both sexes.

The Lounge Lizards.

"Echar la hueva." Another derivation of huevos used for the lounge lizards, this means to laze around or to slack off. "Me da hueva," "It gives me eggs!" So I don't feel like doing it. "Tengo hueva" "I have the lazies and don't feel like doing it." Huevon. Lazy and useless bum. "A huevo." When forced to do something. "Lo hizo de huevos" Proving one's machismo by doing something you wouldn't normally do. "Me lo paso por los huevos." Recounting your superiority, Like, "He's so insignificant, he passed underneath my balls!"

Ahem…Fucking (over) and Being Fucked (over).

CHINGON. Many expletives use derivatives of the word "Chingar," or to "Fuck" someone. A person can often be described, with no little admiration, as "Muy chingon" "A real motherfucker, or stud" with overtones of machismo. To chinge someone, along with machismo itself, began in the days of the Conquest and is beyond the scope of this handbook. The term can also be applied to cars or any object of great desire. Also heard more often today is "Machin," taken from the English and used as a term of approbation, "Este coche es muy machine, "This is a baaad car, bro!" Chingar is also used as "Fuck!" (Usually and more politely, "Coger"). The omnipresent "Chingar tu madre," "Fuck you mother," should be avoided by strangers as it's a top insult, along with "Hijo de la puta" "Son of a whore." "Cabron," "Bastard," and others you will come across. Although milder, "Idiota," similar to the English "Idiot" should be avoided, it is more of an insult here. "Tonto" is milder and common, like our "Twit," more or less.

He or She is a Real Turn-On!

"Prender" is the verb for turn or switch on - commonly used for the lights. So a person or thing "Muy prendido" it really pulls my chain, babe! This seen as a stronger way to use the tradition, "Gustar," "Me gusta mucho," "I Like him or her a lot."

Take it Easy, Mon!

"Tranquilo." Gringos who get easily upset will soon be advised by an in-control Mexican to "Tranquilate," This doesn't quite mean the same as the English "Tranquil," as we don't use it as a command, just a state. In Mexico it means merely "Take it easy, bro," and is meant kindly.

What a Bummer!

"Gacho." A street word now in common usage to describe anything "ugly," (normal Spanish usage, "feo."). The expression "Que gacho" means a "bummer," "No seas gacho," is don't be, ugly, uncool - a spoil-sport.
"Fuchi." A close relative of gacho, and usually used by women, along with the expressive "Wacala!" indicates something is repulsive and stinks. Like our "Yuck."

More Slang Used in Everyday Life.

Apart from slang to convey all of the sex, drugs and rock 'n' roll, Mexico has a lot of tried and true ways of saying quite ordinary things that are a departure from text book Spanish.

"Orale" give, take or let's go, etc. "Orale," ya, vamonos a bailar" let's go! To the dance.
"Andale" Used as "orale" 90% Also as "who are you kidding!"

"Ajuaa and Yahuaaa" Very Mexican cry of delight, often heard among tipsy in cantinas.

"Hijole" Like "shit, no!" an expression used in dismay at unhappy happenings.

"Fregado" something is undone, a nuisance or broken (also "chingado" and "jodido")

"Chido" cute, pretty.

"Gacho" ugly, unpleasant

"Neta" formal "verdad" truth

"Bronca" very common for fight or argument

"No hay pax" (or paz) Probably short for "porque" to say no problem. Note: "paz" also means peace.

"Que pax" are you looking for problems? A fight?

"A poco" one of the commonest phrases in Mexican slang, usually used by women. It means "En serio?" are you serious…you're not kidding.

"Chance" an opportunity "Dame chance" give me the opportunity

"De perdida" at least…at the very least, normally "de menos?"

"Jalada" a joke in bad taste

"Pendejo" A ferocious insult in Spanish…Stupid! Idiot! Asshole!

"Mamada" a nonsense, a stupidity ("tonteria" Lit.)

"No mamas" Lit. don't suck me, used to say don't pull my leg…don't say or do stupid things

"Naco" a word like "Nigger" in English. To be avoided by foreigners and used as an insult to poor, uneducated Indians who may, or may not, be behaving badly. Also used by one "Naco" as a derogatory term for another. (Like Nigger or "Beaner" is in the USA)."Latir" also "Gustar" to like someone or something.

"Chorro" gossip…empty conversation

"Punal" effeminate person (mariquita) a little queer – faggot.

"Cuate" Very common for close friend "El es mi cuate" he is my friend. Also "carnal" "amigocha" etc., etc.

"Gringo" Sure you must know this one! Once a rather offensive term for a North American, now in more general use, but is still rather impolite unless the folks are well known to one another (Like "beaner")

"Madrazo" A hard slap or blow to the face…used also as a threat ("golpe" formal)

"Metiche" Nosey. Used to describe me at various times by assorted girl friends.

"Chisspiss" a cute and sibilant interjection heard a lot that means ""Shhh!" or "Pssst" also stands alone as an interjection.

"Ton" take a car or taxi

"Carro" also "coche" car

Lighten Up Bro'.

"Pesado." One of my favourite all time Mexican words. It means heavy, literally, and can be used for that, "Este paquete es muy pesado." "This packet is very heavy." But it is also well used to describe one who is acting in a boring way: a "drag," or "creep." "Callate, eres mu pesado." "Shut up, and lighten up."

What a Bloody Creep!

"Sangron." "Sangre" means "blood" in Spanish, so "Sangron," or "Sangrona," for the woman, means acting in a "bloody" way, just as in English, except no noun is qualified.

ENGLISH SAYINGS IN MEXICAN SPANISH

A Foxy Chick – A Cute Dude (Fella').

"Guapo" is handsome (guapa for a girl). Adding "Que onda, guapo?" means "what's happening, handsome?" "Hola guapas" (Pl.) does as a gallant and magnanimous salute...after all, aren't all the ladies handsome? (pretty)..well, you can pretend, can't you!? Other adjectives that can be changed from masqueline ("o" ending in most cases), to feminine ("a" ending generally) are: "Lindo" "Bonito," also a fish), "chula," (not "chulo" in this case). Women can be cute, "preciosa," or "mona" pretty, the traditional (and lovely) "bella," beautiful, "primarosa,"
Attractive women are called: "cuerito" "buenola" "curvy." "guitarra," (from the instrument's shape), and "mango." Some with rather more graphic tone are "buen culito (good piece of ass), " and more found in any standard dictionary. Mexicans have many "flors," or flowers, which they deliver with varying degrees of acceptance to the current apple of their eye, who may be any passing female. If the lady is you, ignore these completely; acknowledging a flor may be seen as a come-on to the Mexican macho. Some of these flors are "Hola muneca" (or munecita), hello little doll. "Hola mi vida, mi alma, mi corazon": Hello my life, my soul, my heart...etc, their are literally thousands well-tried and invented on the spot. I overheard one Mexican lovingly hurling a flor "Hola alacrancito que ha picado mi corazon." "Hello little scorpion who has pierced my heart." An accepted and rather sweet part of Mexican street life.

Men can be referred to as "Cuadrado," meaning well-built, or buffed. Women often hear "Sancudo," Daddy-long-legs, an obvious analogy (also heard delivered with some irony to a chick under 4 feet tall!). The parts of the anatomy of the ladies admired by men are : Those with large tits, "Chichonas" (chichis are tits). "Nalgonas," those with a good plump butt, and another, along with sancudo, for the long-legged sorority "Piernuda," leggy. So far, I haven't heard a man's "Lunch-box" described in Spanish, but I am sure it is out there - may I suggest, "Salchichon," having a large sausage!...any treatise of Mexican slang can only by definition skim the surface; new words and phrases appear almost daily.

The Money Honey.

The ubiquitous word that began on the border and spread south many years ago for money is "Feria." If you're short of the necessary, say, "No tengo feria," "I haven't any (or insufficient) bread." You will see Mexican women running for the hills! Just as common in DF and other points south is "Lana." Means wool, but is more likely a diminutive of "Porcelana." "Plate" is used throughout the Spanish speaking world and may mean money in general, or coin of the particular realm in which it is used. "Pesos," in Mexico, for example. Everyone in the world wants US dollars, so much so, that you may here Mexicans saying "Cuanto en Ingles?" "How much in English?" (money)...Dollars they mean, Stirling or Euros are not welcomed outside of the banks yet in Mexico. "De lana" means "Of money," meaning a person is rich. A rich chick, then, is a "Torta de lana," (a sandwich of money). And all the men called Ricardo in Mexico either blanche or swell with pride when they hear the rich being called "Ricardos," slang for the well heeled.

Whores, Cuckolds and Assorted "Cabrons!

"Puta." A whore, politely, "Prostituta," becomes "Puta" on the streets or in the cantinas. And Puta added to other words or endings enriches the language no end!
"Puta!!" "You're shitting me!!"
"Puta madre!" Fuck this shit!"
"Emputarse" Loosing your rag. (along with "Emputar")
"No tengo ni un puta peso!" "I don't have a friggin dime!"
"Putear" What formal folk will do when they read this: Bitch!
"Cabron" To repeat, a word used carefully here because of its overtones of weak male sexuality.
Literally, "El Cabron" is a man who allows himself to be cuckolded, an unhappy state ingrained in the Mexican psyche since the Spanish Conquest, when the invaders took the Indian's wives by force. Which is why visitors to Mexico need tread very carefully when courting local women. This applies equally to women who are separated, or even legally divorced; the ex. macho may still forbid any union, especially with a Gringo, to the point of violence to both parties. Your author has had first- hand experience of this!
"Que cabron!" An intense happening.
"Estuvo cabron el examen." The test was a bitch.

""Encabronarse." Get very worked up.
"Encabronear." It pissed me off.
Cabron can also be used to express approval or even heavy mate-ship:-
"El es un cabron!" (said admiringly) He is a good fighter, lover, what have you.
"Oye cabron!" An address to a close friend. (careful!)
In fact, cabron or "Buey," (Ox, meaning homeboy) are used about every other word by Mexican working class males.
"Se lastimo, pero carbon!!" He/she was very badly injured (or emotionally hurt).
"Soy un cabron!" Along with "Soy un chingon!" (I'm a stud/fighter, etc). This - "I'm a cabron," means the speaker is a hell of a bad dude! And to strut his stuff like this, he might well be (or more commonly legless).

The World's a Gas!

El Pedo. Literally, "A fart." As you might gather, all the meanings of words using "Pedo" in them indicate problems. We seem to have missed a golden opportunity in English here!
"Estoy pedo." "I'm legless."
"Es todo un pedo." This situation is really screwed up.
"Tengo pedos con mi mujer." "I'm fighting with the main squeeze."
"Que pedo?" What's going on?"
"Ponarse una peda." To get drunk as a sailor. (Also "empedarse").

Moctezuma's Revenge.

To "Andar con el cutis flojo" (Walk with slack skin) means you have diarrhea, a common complaint in Mexico..
But "Andar con mal tapon" (Walk with a bad stopper, or cork) The opposite, you're bunged up!
(This is also used to say someone is "Uptight.")
All problems associate with your "Aniz" Lit. "anus" as in English.
And not getting to the toilet in time might leave you "Apedrear," Reeking of shit!
(This also means to "Stone to death," In this case, the root, "ped..." is from "PiEDras," (rocks) " not "PEDo" (fart).
Finally, the description rendered to this writer nowadays, "Pinche Viejo pedoro" "Fucking old fart!"

More on Finance.

The down payment. Known as an "Enganche," (Lit. Hook), what you might pay to layaway an item. Many places still have the charming tradition of the "Pilon" a little extra, although the habit is dying as Mexico catches up with the greedy manner of the First World. (I had a furious argument with an employee over a penny in England a couple of years back when the bill was £100 and one penny and asked to be excused the penny! No way, Jose!). Big supers in Mexico like Aurrera and Gigante used to have free titbits everywhere 20 year ago, but hardly ever in 2005. To "Doy Pilon" means to give more for the money, but another book on slang says a bandit once said he gave

Pilon when he pumped an extra bullet into a corpse! Hardly the general philosophy associated with the term. (A prostitute might use pilon when she says she also gave the customer venereal disease!). Other mobster induced sayings might be ""Caifas," Pay up, and "Caifas con me lana" or "azote con me lana" Pay up or face the consequences.

Sweat of the Brow and Debts.

To work is "Trabaja," but we also hear "Chamba" "Chamba," or "Jale" is the job or gig. Kid's pocket money is paid on Sunday and is therefore the "Domingo." Drugs are "Drogas," but debt is also "Droga," maybe because it becomes a habit. "Droguero" and "Endrogada" are themes along the lines of debt ridden as well as high on drugs. To be broke is "Pelado," Peeled, "Jorobado," Hunchbacked, down and out, (very illustrative of how we slouch when we're short of the necessary!). Also "Quinta," "En la quinta," or "No tengo ni una quinta." Without a cent. "Alimentos" Lit. Food, or food allowance. Also used for alimony.

Gimme a Break, Bud!

Commonest way to ask for breathing space is "Dame chanza." On the street you will also hear "alvianame," usually used when borrowing or hustling something. Recent addition was "Mochete," as in to mooch. "No seas gacho, carnal," "Be a sport, homeboy,"

Sex, Drugs and Other Foibles.

Nowhere, sadly we suppose, is street slang in any language so rich as when dealing with sex, drugs or the often revolting habits found among Homo sapiens: Man. You will never, we hope, need to use it all and possibly never have to hear it, especially if it is directed at you.

The Penis.

The English language is said to have close to 100 words for the male organ. The inventive Mexican would not fall far short (no pun intended). The conventional term is "Pene." Cock, or Prick in English would translate as "La verga." This is actually part of the rigging of a ship and used as a separate swear word. An erection, or "hard-on" is "verga dura," or "parado." When the Mexican transport minister included the term, "Precaution, paradas continuas" inside all the buses, it caused no end of merriment. As well as warning of frequent stops, the term could be taken as meaning, "Careful frequent erections!"
Another well used and common penistic analogy is the ubiquitous "Chile." As well as adding spice to most Mexican dishes, the chile enhances many jokes and puns. Common is for a wag to ask a visitor, blandly, "Te gusta chile?" "SI" responds the hapless victim, "I love chiles!" Much merriment all around. Having a large chile is "Chiludo," and, yes, it means well-hung.
Here are some of the others in common usage:-
 "Pajaro," Bird.
"Pito,"   Whistle (Common)

"Pinga" (Dick)
"Baston" Cane
Bastardo, Carnado (Bait)
Perno Spike
Pistola and Rifle (used in jokes)
"Chorizo" (Thick, pork sausage)
"Elote" Maize cob
"Hueso" Bone
"Pipi (small dick)...also "Chilito." Care here, this is also a food item at Taco Bell!
"Lechero" Gives "milk!"
The fascinating ""Chuperson!"
"Miembrillo" Limb.
"Morrongo."
My personal favourite "Mazacuata," A snake from Guerrero!
There are many more, but this should see you through!
A popular joke is to ask another unsuspecting Gringo if he knows the puros (cigars) from Campeche (State to the south). Wanting to appear one of the boys, although having not heard of the said cheroot, which do not exist, the Gringo replies "Yes, they are very good" To which the couplet is finished like this: "No sale humo, sale leche!" (which rhymes with 'Campeche') In other words, the victim has replied that, yes, he loves the "cigar" which doesn't smoke, it "comes!" Much amusement all round.

Having a Ball with Slang.

Much hilarity is enjoyed by working class Mexicans who hear you ask for "Huevos Mexicanos" for breakfast. You might get asked - as has happened to me before I got wise - "Why, what's wrong with yours?" Huevos (eggs) are also slang for testicles and you just asked the waiter if you might have some Mexican Balls. (along with "aguacates," (avocados) "albondigas," (meat balls), "ayotes," pumkins, "chayotes," (gourds), "auayon torneados," "cojones," Etc.). The correct way to ask for the common breakfast dish is "Juevos a la Mexicana," or Eggs done Mexican style.

But so important to the Mexican street macho is his balls, that they are exalted.

"Sopladores" things that blow (soplar) testicles
"Tompeates" Same
"Ayotes" pumkins.
"Tanates" balls
"Mecos" and "Mermelada de miembrillo" (fruit jam) semen cum
"Obstaculos" obstacles balls

Leave it to Beaver!

The polite term, as in English, is "Vagina." Our "pussy," or "beaver," is the word "Panocha," which is actually unrefined brown sugar or a sweet bread. "Pucha" is c---t and also used as a sharp oath. As most words by all sexual organs are invented by Mexican machos, other terms for the female "paradise valley" are rather affectionate and amusing. Such as "La Cucaracha," Yes, that's your little cockroach, honey. "Sarten," Frying Pan, a little obscure. The graphic "Lunar Peludo," or hairy birthmark! "Bizcocho" biscuit. "Mondongo, paparrucha and concha" all sea creatures. "Argolla," is the term for the hymen, used as we use "cherry."

Also:-
"Mamey" a fruit and "Remame" from the same source
"Bacalao" codfish.
"Chocho"...also means "an old person ready for the reaper!
"Nido" Little bird's nest or hiding place.

Tits or Breasts.

The most formal term is "Senos" Careful here. The current abbreviation for both senoritas and senoras is also "Senos." Then, conceivably, "Mira los senos con los senos!" "Look at the chicks with the tits!" The chest, or breast, is correctly called "Pecho" and breast are "pechitos." The sexy "Chichis" is the commonest street term. One with large bust, then, is a "Chichona."
Other terms are:-
"Chimeneas" chimneys.
"Peras" pears.
"Agarraderas," (Underground train hanging straps!)
"Repistas" shelves.
"Alimentos" Nourishment.
"Defensas" Bumpers.
"Educcacion" ("She had a real good education!")
Other terms making the rounds are :_
"Manchas" Also means a spot or stain and also "wet paint."
"Colgadas" Hanging...a woman with withered "old tits"
Leave it, she's someone's mum, wife, or sister.

The Bottom (Bum, or Ass).

Mexicans say "Tits are for babies, bums are for men." Which does fit in with what the animal kingdom finds attractive, in many species.

Most common is the word for buttocks, "Nalgas." Streetier is "Las nachas." Polite and usual used by women is "Pompis" A curvaceous butt is a "Zalate." "Cola," is tail. So "Besame culo" is "Kiss my ass!" "Calabazo" The rump.

The anus gets a lot of attention in Mexico (although much less in a homosexual context...to be gay here is unfortunate: to be referred-to as "queer," when you are not is fighting talk).

Physiologically, the anus is "ano," profanely, "Cono," or "Culo"(the former used like "buey" ox affectionately among friends, or as an insult to others - mainly in Spain).

Also "El chico," the little one.

"El polar sur," the South Pole.

"Ojete" Very common as curse and in graffiti (written "OGT")

There is no actual term for "Assholes" as in the USA. Neither so they have the common expressions "To kick ass," "Piece of ass," etc.

To paddle someone is "Nalgada".

"Trasero" rear end or butt

"Differencial" like in a car for a shapely female derriere.

"Mapa mundi" world map is equivalent to our "moon."

"Cucu." Sexy, modish and musical, the female anus.

As in popular song "No te metas con mi cucu" (Don't get into my booty!")

Also:-
"Aniz anus"
"El de atras" "He at the back!" Asshole! Also "trastero" Lit. storeroom.
"Zurramato" A dumbass! Also applied to a whole host of undesirable characteristics as perceived by the Mexican street boy: Stupid, lazy, ugly, etc.

Making Love....or merely Screwing. (Shagging, UK!)

Mexico has all the equivalents of fucking, screwing, shagging, banging, et al, that we find in the Anglo tongue. (It amazed me to find "having a shag" in the UK today is used as casually as having a meal!). Here are most of them and more arrive yearly, which is why books like this eventually become just curiosities. Many slang words, though, eventually become part of the culture and survive for centuries.

"Amor," of course, is "love" and making love "haciendo la amor." But this isn't street and your "cuate" best bud would scorn you for saying your girl and you did that last night. Save the conventions for when you are with the ladies or the family.
"Bastardiar" and "Bombear" To have sex outside of marriage - and, yes, the first expression means "To produce a bastard!"
"Echar un palo" throw the stick.
"Medir su aceite" Literally, "Check her oil!"
"Darle a comer el chango" feed the monkey.
"Revisar los interiores" check out her interior.
"Subir el guayabo" climb the guayabo tree.

"Andar por caderas" walk on the hips.
"Mojar el barbon" wet the bearded one.
"Tomar medias por dentro" take interior measurements.
"Tronar los huesitos" rattle her bones.
"Aplicar inyeccion intrapiernosa" Administer an 'interlegular' injection. (Good example of a contrived word).
"Reunir los ombligos" reunite (join) bellybuttons.
"Cuchi-cuchi" and "riqui-rique" For the 'cute' set, means making it.
"Colchanazo" A raging fuck, literally, "attacking the mattress."
"Ir a degastar el petate" To wear down the bedding.
"Ir a desvencigar el cama" Go break the bed.
"Ir a hacer de las aguas" Go and make some water.
"Ir a la junta de consiliation" Lit. go to a meeting. Note: "Consiliation" is also the labor court in Mexican towns and cities and where a complaining worker goes for relief.
"Ir a la lucha super libre a calzon" rip the gear off and dive in!
"Ir a percudir el colchon" to tarnish the mattress.
"Ir a rechinar la cama" to make the bed squeak.
And finally, perhaps aping the French definition of life after orgasm, "Le petit mort" little death.
"Ir a un entierro" Go to the grave!
To remove the hymen is "Hacer un favor" do a favor, one for the feminists! "Tronar el parche" blow the patch,
"Romper el tambor" rip the drum, "Dejar sin cosita" leave her without her little thing, "Descorchar" pull the cork.

The Hated Sheath.

The church and state have been separated for more than 100 years in Mexico so there is little effective opposition by the church towards contraception. AIDS and assorted pathogenic horrors have struck Mexico as well over the last 20 years and the rubber has become an important adjunct to life, advertised everywhere and - reluctantly by machos - used. Along with the increase in the need for contraception, especial the ubiquitous rubber, has risen the street idiom.

The rubber is properly known as the "Condon" only the final "n" making the word different from English and many other lands. Also heard is the other polite word, "Preservativo" and as it might indeed "preserve" your life, this word has taken on a new meaning in this millennium. And "Impermeable" raincoat. Although reluctantly used, they will never be loved, hence the sobriquet "Diablito" little devil, or "desafinador" the "untuner."

Others heard around are:-
"Portalapiz" pencil box
"Prudencia" lady Prudence (used with prudence!)
"Sombrero de Panama" Panamanian hat
"Paragua" umbrella...literally "for water"
"Globito or bomba" Both Spanish for balloons
"Caperucita en carnada" capped bait
"Angel de la Guardia and Angel Custodia" both mean Guardian Angel
"El sin mangas" he without his hose
"Tacuche de Filiberto" tacuche is a garment and Filiberto is a man's name and also slang for dick...not surprisingly, Filiberto has waned as a popular name at

Christening time!
"Manga" various meanings, including the female of "mango," a sexy man.

Masturbation: Jerking-Off, Wanking, et al.

Not unlike Anglo lands, masturbation is not a topic readily advanced in conversation. Men who masturbate are seen as losers; the real macho has as much "panocha" (pussy) as he wants, (or says he does). Women undoubtedly relieve themselves in the same was their Anglo cousins do, but you won't ever hear about it from them in Mexico. And, in fact, they probably do it less than in sex-obsessed countries such as England.

In Mexico, men who masturbate literally make a fist of it. "Puni" (poon yee) or fist forms the root of many expressions. Hence "Punetazo" and "Hace la puneta" with connotations of blows and shotguns. The one I have heard the most is "Paja," straw, or "Hacer paja" make like straw. Used like jacking-off in the USA. A "punetero," or "pajero" (bird) is someone with Portnoy's Complaint, a constant wanker. The ladies, delicately, are referred-to as "doing it with the finger," even if these days they use 14 inches of frantic plastic..."dedear" covers this. After all, ponders the macho, "Is she thinking of me while she's doing it?"

Some more terms being handed around (pun intended) are these:-

"Vergalito" Jerking off your little chicken! Derived from "verga" dick and "gallo" cock..."ito" added to denote smallness.

"Vergallo" Similar. When describing this to another, a

macho may do a little dance flapping his arms and crowing while simulating masturbation. Tough when "barracho" (drunk)
"Avergallon." Derivation of above.
Real cocks look on smugly, they usually have many hens to take care of.

More on whores, ("putas") and Brothels, (bordellos).

If you go with a "Chucha cuerera" you have unearthed a very experienced woman who may or may not charge you.
"Puta" hooker who will charge…rate is usually up for negotiation
"Abedesa" pimp, male or female
"Aduana" Lit. Customs…slang, whore house
"Tana" prostitute
"Rule" (ruh lay") a hardened whore, also "Ruletera
"Taconera" a whore who moves around (from place to place, not as in writhing!) This term is taken from "Taconear" to fill or stuff
"Retozona" whore, a play on "frisky" and the Zona (below)
"Madama" whore house head, also "Madre superior!" mother superior
"Madrota" and "Madrina." Note: The derogatory terms employ use of the "Madre" or mother again.
"Berreadero" brothel
"La Zona Rosa," or simply, "Zona." Place in many Mexican towns where the legalized whores hang out. Well policed with (more of less) clean girls whom can be had cheaply (and even more cheaply as the night

wears on). They can be fun if caution is employed. Beer is quite cheap, the music is free and if you can resist the pressure to buy the girls drinks (phoney and dear) you can have a cheapish night out.

Homosexuals.

As in English, "homosexual" is the technical and polite word for those of this persuasion. "Gay" has replaced most other terms in general use, pronounced "guy" in Mexico. Gays do not have quite the cachet they seem to have aquired in the US and UK. But there is little real "gay bashing" amongst these generally gentle and understanding folk. In fact, there is much more teasing of one another with homosexual innuendo by blue collar Mexicans than is found among Anglo workers. Strange, really, in a place where machismo is still a force to be reckoned with…perhaps the cool acceptance of the jibes and the quick, smiling counters actually enforce masculinity?

Lesbians, apart from the percentage of "bull dyke" types, are much more low-key. Only in show business, as everywhere, do lesbians and male homosexuals enjoy freedom of lifestyle and expression. As in our culture, several terms for 'queers and 'faggots are still in common usage.

One of Mexico's leading lesbians in the 70's through the 90's was the US writer, Pat Nelson. I worked with Pat for some years at the Mexico City News (Now sadly defunct). She threw great parties and once confided in me that she had seduced all the beautiful actresses of her time in Mexico!

Here are some of the terms for Gays you might hear:_

"Joto" fairy or flit, the lingua standard. Not really polite, in fact rather insulting.

"Puto" like faggot, (from the female "Puta" whore). Very rude term and used with care.

"Puton" a flaming faggot!

"Maricon" standard term for an effeminate man. But also used affectionately by women to their men…make sure she's kidding!

"Marimacha" Rarely used: means butch, as in dyke.

"41" "cuarenta y uno in speech. For homos in general (opposite of "14" "catorce" to mean "sex" or "fuck")

"De los otros" and "aves raros," "the others," and "rare birds" said about gays in general as being different from "us."

"Jugar en dos campos" play on both sides, like "ac-dc" for bi-sexuals.

AIDS is SIDA in Spanish: those suffering from the affliction are "sidosos"

(Maybe we could have "bandaids!")

"Mayate" faggot

"Quebracho" and "quebrachon"

Lit. broken..homosexuals.

Drugs: Marijuana, Heroin, Cocaine, etc.

Drugs occupy an uneasy position in Mexico. The US is leaning hard on the country to control the flow of illegal substances to the north. Superficially, the authorities are "Hard" on those in possession of even small amounts of cannabis. Yet police have been easily bought off with a mordida. On the other hand, foreigners have languished in prison for many months waiting to get the process to act for them, often for small amounts of a drug that would have brought them a smack on the hand in the States. Don't get involved, is sane advice: in drugs or in firearms.

"Mota" ...pot, or weed, is the commonest term for cannabis (marijuana).

"Yierba" or "Yerba" (yair bah) is often heard. Cannabis has been part of the culture here for hundreds of years and many are the words to describe it.

Plays on "mota" like "motocicleta," "motives," Some terms began as grower's names, such as "oro de Acapulco," Acapulco gold. "rojo de Oaxaca," Oaxacan Red.* "de la Buena," the good stuff, or "clorofila de la verde" the green stuff. "fina esmerelda" the fine stuff, ("Hey, man, ain't it all!). You may hear "coliflor tostada" toasted cauliflower. "Oregano Chino" Chinese oregano, ""zacate Ingles" English hay, "doralilla" little golden, "dona diabla" devil woman, "dama de la ardiente caballera" lady of the horny hair-do. "nalga de angel" angel ass, "trueno verde" green thunder, "motor de chorro" jet engine.

Those using the evil weed in Mexico , the "heads" if you like, are "marihuanos," they "burn" (quemar) or "toast," (tostar) the grass to smoke it. A pun on "mota" is "motorizar" motorize; "dorar" add golden gilt (maybe where Acapulco gold originated).

Other terms heard frequently are:-
"Enyerba" to herbify
"Enamoriscar" to cover with love, (after amor, love)
"Mordisquear" to take a nibble (toke), also "aceleron") accelerate.
The English "Joint" is formally "cigarro" cigarette, but also ""porro" and the roach or nub is a "bachicha."
Of interest may be where the English "toke" originated.

It was certainly from the Spanish "to touch" "tocar." Head talk is "Te toca," "it touches you" as the joint is passed around.

Here are a few more terms often applied to the "evil weed," so deeply ingrained in the culture here:-

"Chora" marijuana
"Aracata" Same
"Atizar" To smoke weed
"Acostarse con Rosemaria" Lit. To sleep with Rosemary also smoke weed
"Grifear" smoke wee
"Grifo" Drug-induced state…usually high on weed
"Moravia" weed
"Morisqueta" weed
"Motivosa" weed
"Motor de chorro" weed
"Toca la Nalga de un angel" Lit. Angels's buttock! Smoke weed
"Oregano" Common slang for weed

Smoking Tobacco

Mexicans smoke less than we do, especially the women, who generally may smoke and drink only socially, often passing a cigarette around the coffee clatch like a joint. The obsessive smoking, as found in Europe amongst females, is hardly seen amongst Mexican women (nor the lager loutesses!): A women seen drunk on the streets in Mexico is extremely rare outside of the D.F. where anything goes. Mexican men of the peon class also smoke less, but more in cities: in the Rural sector, there is little money available for vices.

"Frajo" like the British "fag" (awful word) is the commonest street term for a ciggie. Oldsters still use "chiva" (and "chevi" is common for a beer). The Anglo "coffin nails" has its equivalent in "tacos de cancer!" (like the skinny, tightly rolled tacos known as "flautas," often served with pozole). Cigars are known as "puros" and Mexico has very good cigars: the leaf is grown and the cigars made in the tropical south of Veracruz State…an area well worth a visit for cigars and the huge and beautiful Catemaco Lake, a center of witchery in Mexico!

Cocaine: "Blow," "The Lady," "Nose Candy," etc.

"Cocaina" is cocaine and called "coca" on the street. The beverage, Coke, is also coca, but the environment while ordering should determine what you receive!

Heroin, "Smack," etc.

"Narcotrafficantes" drug traffickers (narcos) call heroin "chiva" goat. Among many other terms are:-
"Nieve, Cura, Medicina,Dona Blanca, etc.
Mexican brown heroin is known as ""chicloso de Mandarin" Madarin chewing-gum; "Chocolate Chino" Chinese chocolate, or the ubiquitous "Chinaloa" a hybrid of China and Sinaloa, which has the doubtful distinction on being Mexico's leading drug state.
Some other terms for this debilitating drug:-
"Gumersinda" raw heroin, or crude opium
"Chinaloa Opium" as above
"Chocolate de Fu Man Chu" opium or pure heroin.

Drugs can spell Trouble for Visitors

Mexico's drug laws are not as liberal, especially where pot is concerned, as they are in many states of the US, or even in Europe, as we see countries like Britain taking a much softer approach to "soft" drugs and even easing penalties and quantities for possession of "Class A" substances. And not to be forgotten when skating on this thin ice with the law is the "Mordida" or bite. This is the non-official "fine" imposed by police for all sorts of offences. And where flouting a minor traffic law will only result in a few dollars "bite," getting arrested for possession can result in fines, both imposed by arresting officers, or the courts, of thousands. And you may find yourself in jail while the money is raised.

The Fuzz.

So hated police and incarceration are well covered in the slang department:-
"Policia" or "Patrulla" both like to be referred-to as "Officials" officer.
Sometimes they are called "Placas" or badges. You may hear "Jaiba" crab, "Azul" blue - like our boys in blue. Traffic cops get called "Lobos" wolves, or "Feroz" fierce. A cop on the take (most are...their salaries are ridiculous) is a "Mordilon" and the paddy waggon is the "Julia."

Prison, Jail - the Slammer

Ending in prison is the "carcel" or "calabozo" jail. Also "Tambo" or "Bote"
"La peni" from the formal "Penitenciaria." Also "La Pinta," taken from the expression "Hacer la pinta" or play hookey from school.

COMMUNICATING WITH FAMILY AND FRIENDS

The Kiddiewinks

It's no secret that Mexicans love their children and put them before anything, period. You notice this in shops where attendants take no notice of you until the child they are serving is happy, no matter how long it takes. There are few incidences of petty cruelty there: slapping, nagging, pushing or pulling. Kids are welcome everywhere and no attempt is made to segregate them. Any establishment barring children would soon go out of business in Mexico. Parents know when places or events are not suitable for kids and act accordingly.

Many of the words in common usage for youngsters simply mean "the little one." Such as "chico" "chiquito" or "pequeno" (with "a" for female child).

"Chamaco" general word for kids and one sometimes used scoldingly "Ya! Chamaco!" enough, son! Newer is "buki" after the singing group of that name. Babies will often take the Italian "bambinos" in Mexico.

North Mexico hosts the term "plebe" for baby, brat, kid, etc. A real monter could be called "travieso" mischievous, or "esquincle" brat. And don't you just love "mocoso" snot-nose! A bogey is a moco here.

Lovers "Amantes"
Street talk: "huesos" (bones), "varedas" (paths?) and "patos" (ducks)
Affectionate terms for women (They are legion!) "muneca" (doll), "munequita" (little doll), "preciosa"

(precious…for either sex), also "tesoro," my treasure, "ricura" my richness, "chiquetin" my little darlin', Formal are "mi amor" my love, "mi vida," my life, "mi corazon" my heart, etc. are all used for any member of the family and some close friends.

Women often call their husbands and male kids, "papi," or "papito" for little daddy…also "mami" and "mamita" for the females.

"Viejo" is the standard name for an old man, or the old man (spouse). Same with "vieja" for the missus. An interesting derivation is "mi peor es nada" Lit. my worst is nothing, but used to say, better than nothing.

Machos may denigrate the main squeeze by referring to her as a "Detalle" detail, "figura" a figure even "pescado" fish! Love affairs "adventuras amorosas" reach the street as "volados" flyers, "aguacates" avocados, "volantinos" and "movidas" (perhaps from "mi vida" above).

"Coquetear" Lit. flirt, street, "volarse" they fly, also "andar de volado" volado means suddenly, but the phrase means to flirt.

You will also hear:-

"Dar puerta" give the door

"Dar entrada" give out passes or tickets

"Pelar las dientes" peel the teeth (lovely; the crocodile smile of the seductor!)

"Hacer el iris" do the iris - the eyes down comeon

"Mover el agua" stir the water

"Levantar polvo" raise dust - maybe that was in the days of the Mexican cowboy, the charro as he spurred his horse towards town.

"Echar los perros" for female flirts who are tossing a dog to the favored one!

Family Members

"Padres," or "Papas" Lit. parents. But referred-to as "viejos" everywhere.
Also "mi jefes" my bosses "Viejo" or "vieja" singular is not used to refer to individual parents, but "jefa" boss, fem, replaces "Viejo" Slang words for mama or mami are "Mandonna" a play on "mandon" one who orders and "Madonna" the Virgin. Also with religious connotations mum gets called "Angustiada" anguished.
"Primo" or "prima" is cousin, but can be used to refer to a country cousin, as in English, a hick.
"Suegra" beloved or hatred, the ubiquitous mother-in-law! She is a figure of fun and jokes as in English but with perhaps a lot more influence.
"Abuela(o)" grandma or grandad…doesn't Spanish save a lot of time by using a masqueline or feminine word ending, "a" or "a?" But this can be very confusing for foreigners who often never learn them all. I mean, "el dia" the day, masqueline, but "la noche" the night, feminine. There are many more apparently random rulings.

Everyday Words Borrowed by Slang.

As in the English, "Hell," often not PC in polite company and changed to "Heck," Mexicans do the same with their words and phrases, but far more frequently. After all, manners count far more here and one insults with care.
"No mames" Lit. don't suck, but used for don't bullshit (me), be serious.
Change 1 "No manches" Lit. don't stain, but replaces above in meaning

Change 2 "No mamey" the mamay is a sweet fruit
"Esta cabron!" that's intense (uses offensive cabron word)
Change "Esta canon" not vulgar
"A huevo" hell, yeah! (although huevo is egg)
Change 1 "A hueso" hueso is bone
Change 2 "A Wilbur" seen as comical and phonetically similar
"Un acido" an acid, tab of LSD
Change "Un ajo" clove of garlic (change for disguise)
"Algo" some…somewhat
Change "Algodon" cotton or cotton candy
"Mota" marijuana (cannabis, weed)
Change "Moronga" a blood sausage like Haggis
"Sacate la mota" break out the weed
Change "Sacaracate la maracachimba" Lit ? poetic and funny
"Que milagro que te dejas ver" what a miracle to see you!
Change "Que milanesas que te dejas bisteces" what breaded steak that you let yourself steak! Nutty and funny in today's patois.
"A su madre" Lit. to his mother, slang: hol shit! Etc.
Change 1 "A su mecha" to his lamp wick
Change 2 "A su maquina" to his machine…Huh? Yeah, we know! And you thought London Cockneys were confusing.
"Que onda?" what's happening? ("Onda" is a strange word that no one can satisfactorily translate means "what thing," approximately.)
Change "Que hongos?" a hongo ("H" silent in Sp.) is a fungus.
"Que tranza?" what's up? A tranza is an act of putting it over on someone, so the expression means "who

shall we take today" more or less.
Change "Que trampolin" what trampoline
"Que rabo!" Lit. rabbit's scut slang: "What a fox!" (babe, honey, etc.)
Change "Que rabano!" what a radish!
"Esta loco!" He's crazy!
Change 1 "Esta Lorenzo" he's Lawrence!
"Esta bien fea" She's really ugly
Change "Esta bien Federal" (or "Federal Express") a Federal is like FBI

More on Being Cool.

"Cool" The universal approbatory word is "Padre," father, as is mentioned elsewhere in this text. It stands alone, "Que padre!" "How great," or in a sentence, "Es un pelicular muy padre," "What a great film." A more modern street edition of padre is "curado," from "cura" priest or father. Also "suave," literally "smooth," and used as cool.
"Chingon" and "machin" A tough approbation of a "cool" man or machine. "Chido" a recent conversion from gutter talk, chido is nor used for cool or "bitchin" "De pelos" or "de jicamas" recent, rather nutty for cool among the younger set of the capital. (Slang spreads like wildfire).

…And Uncool.

"Gacho" is a word which really sounds like its meaning (many slang words sound like their meaning). Ugly is "feo" but gacho describes any "ugly" things more succinctly.

"Que gacho" a bummer
"Eres gacho" you're an asshole.
"No seas gacho" Don't be an asshole (stinker, cad, meanie, bitch, etc.)
"Pesado" As well as money, peso literally means a weight, and pesado means heavy. But to call someone pesado(a) is to say they are boring, pedantic, a whiner and they should come off it. In other words, they are the opposite of simpatico (above) and are "antipatico." Another derogatory similar term is "sangron" Lit., bloody.
"Chingado" The big "chingar" word, as we have seen above. "estoy chingado" is to mean "I'm screwed!" This term, chingar, and all its derivatives, is buried deep in the Mexican's psyche since the days of the Conquerors when Cortez and his army took any Indian woman they wanted and forced themselves upon her. To chingar was also to rape and the men felt helpless to do anything about it. "Chinga tu madre!" is a strong oath today and probably felt as it was 500 years ago when the Conquistadores violated the mothers, wives and sisters of the peons they ruled.
"Gordo" Literally "fat," but used with caer to express disgust. "El Presidente me cae gordo" "I dislike the President." "Caer mal" is less street.
"Fuchi" Another lyrical word to mean smelly, stinky or generally unacceptable. I have only heard women using this, so it must be less common for men (along with "pipi" for taking a piss!). Also heard "fu" and "furris" Yuck" The turkey-gobble-like "guacala!" is similar; often used when being forced to spit out a mouthful of something, a drunk chucks-up, or the baby's diaper is found to be full of a slimy beige substance, Ugh! guacala!!

Being "Simpatico:" More on Liking and Hating.

"Simpatico." This great old handle, used all over the Spanish speaking world is a "must learn" for anyone visiting Mexico,
It means "nice," but goes beyond this sugar-sweet declaration: Someone simpatico also possesses many characteristics we all admire, such as being good company, warm, caring, amusing and exciting. If a Mexican says you are simpatico, you are on the right track. You are a "gran tipo" or even "tipazo" a good guy. The "izo" on words emphasizes the meaning.
"Caer" Literally, "to fall," If you like someone - he is simpatico you like him or her, "el me cae bien" I like him.
"Gustar" Also expresses approval or liking, but usually reserved for things, me gusta este libro"I like this book. The exception is when expressing sexual interest, but better keep it simple. If something really "turns you on," you might use "prendido" literally, to turn on a light, but used to express strong liking of anything.
"Barbero" Literally, "barbaric," but also used for "cool," or "uncool," rather like the English "baaad, man!"
But "que barbaridad" is always used in the negative, and "una barbarian de" means a lot of something.
"Tranquilo" Another word heard a lot by over-excitable Gringos who are complaining about something. "Why is the darned plumber two weeks late again!?" "Tranquilo," or "Tranquilate" says your Mexican companion, "Take it easy, relax." And the suggestion may have an edge of "we've heard enough!" about it! "Calmada" and "Calmate" is about the same. It might be worth noting that Mexicans, on

the whole, don't get half so het-up about minor setbacks in their lives as many First World residents do. And they tend to look askance at our bootless cries. "So what if the plumber is late," the Mexican ponders, "we have water in the rio, food on the table and the sun is shining." But put Juan behind the wheel of a car and he could teach us all about aggressive driving and road rage. Different ships, different hat tallies, as we said in the Navy. The same applies in restaurants where Mexicans rarely complain about quality, service or price, as North Americans will. They prefer to pay up: shut up, and never go there again…tranquilo…

Humor.

Mexicans love to laugh like jackasses and making someone laugh is a big start in being found simpatico.
"Chiste" is a joke and "chistoso" is comical. "Broma" is a standard word for joke. Dirty jokes are "chistes colorados" and sick jokes are "chistes verdes." A terrible joke which makes you groan is a "raspa" and a pun is "albur."
"Gracioso" This is to be funny "with grace," that is to say, very funny and amusing.
"Vaciado" A "scream" or a "kick," humor-wise.
"Burlar" To kid around and play the fool.
"Picaron" "Picar" is to sting, bite or otherwise attack with a sharp instrument (The "picadors" stick the bull with the lance in the "corrida.")
Hot food, which "bites" the palate is called "picante." As the pica can also be a bird's beak, it is another of the many words for the penis.

In humor, a "picaron" is one who has just caught you napping with a joke or a trick…as in English we have the kid's famous "What's twice the half of two-and-a-half" Hee hee, two-and-a-half, stoopid!"

"Payasear" A "payaso" is a clown, so the above means to do what clowns do, fool around in a manic manner. Teasing women in Mexico will always get "No seas payaso!" Cut out the kidding!

"Caer el Viente" This equals our old "Aha, the coin has finally dropped" when a dim bulb finally gets a joke. The "viente" was the old 20 centavo coin once heard dropping into the old telephones. Caer, of course, is to fall.

"Tomar el pelos" Taking, or pulling the hair: same as "pulling my leg" in English.

"Raro" Means funny peculiar, as "curiosa" is funny weird.

Handsome is as Handsome Does.

"Guapo" is handsome as "guapa" is foxy-pretty. Both are commonly used as a bland address "Hola guapa" hello pretty (women). The person does not have to be attractive to be thus addressed, but he or she might feel her day brightened a bit. "Joven," youngster, is also used as an address for people of any age, although there might be a mildly sarcastic or perhaps encouraging edge to it is the person is obviously over middle age. Many words like this can change the last letter from a "o" to an "a" depending on gender of recipient, but not all do ("cuadrado" for a buffed male is never used for a woman, unless, we imagine, with extreme irony in the case of a female body builder with a preference for her own sex for sex!)

"Cuero" There are many complimentary words in Mexican Spanish for a pretty girl. Cuero is one, including "preciosa, mona, chula, bella, hermosa, primorosa" (gorgeous). Very street are: "cuerita, cuerazo" (referring to shape) also "buenota, Buena curva, guitarra, (guitar-shaped!), and mango," etc. Tepito or back street slang calls good lookers "forro, forazo," and when really emboldened by beer, tequila or pot, Juam might say "buen culito" (nice bum and bits!), "buena percha" (nice tits), "culo chida" really pretty crude but perhaps appreciated by a certain type of girl.

"Sabrosa" Meaning "tasty" this is also thrown into the sexual fray with "potable," (drinkable), "encamable" (beddable), "ensabanable" (under-the-sheets-able!), "revocable" (turnover-able), and the amusing "mordisqueable" (toothsome).

"No sabrosa" The "Ughhh!" factor. (In truth, Mexicans are generally gallant about unattractive ladies, theorizing they are all someone's mum, wife or sister and…with even more verity, they possess the same equipment and you don't have to look at the mantelpiece when poking the only fire running around at 4 am!). So insults there are, but more likely to be used sotto voce among themselves.

"Perita en dulce" pear in syrup, and used like our "sheep in lamb's clothing," Also means a girl way up herself, as the British say, like some of that country's sickening little celebrities with their foul mouths and sluttish, drunken behavior. Plain women are also called "garra, piedra (stone), pellejo" hank of rawhide.

More on the Root of All Evil

"It's money, honey, my little sonny,
And the rich man's joke is always funny."

"Dinero." Money... is perhaps more important to Mexicans than to those in the First World countries, because there is less of it. For the man on the street, it is hard to come by and there is no help at government level. Despite this, Mexicans make light of their financial woes and seem to get by, mainly as a result of family help.
"Feria" The commonest slang word in the Republic for money is feria, having spread from its origins on the US/Mexican border. The word is also used for loose change: beggars are answered thusly "No tengo feria," I have no change. Cheeky hustlers these days have been heard to mutter, "Dame un billete, pues" Give me a bill then! Just as common in the southern half of the country is "lana," literally wool, but it may have its origins in the word "porecelana"
"Plata" silver, is used throughout Latin American countries : "pesos and centavos," of course are the two denominations. Sometimes a price is asked "en Ingles," this meaning in dollars, not Sterling; the British monetary units are practically unknown in Mexico although the Euro is making its presence felt in the Capital.
Other slang words for money include "pachocha, luz and marmaja" but are not commonly heard by foreigners.
"With Money, or Without it, I'll still be King," goes the song, "El Rey," made popular by the great ranchero singer, Vicente Fernandez.

"De lana" means to be rich as a chick with money is called "torta de lana," or wool sandwich. Torta is also one of the slang words for vagina. "Rico," rich, which forms part of the name, "Ricardo," to also mean a richey.

"Sin dinero" is literally without money, but a beggar is a "mendigo," used variously as an insult when the first syllable is emphasized, "MENdigo," son of a bitch.

Using Money.

"Caro" is expensive and "barato" is cheap. As a noun, also "ganga" it indicates a bargain. Also "oferta." "De balde" or "de oquis" means for free . To lay away something, employ the "enganche," down payment. Paying with payments is "en abonos" An enterprising store might give you a "pilon," small bonus or discount.

Although cough is actually "tos," to cough up someone's money is "caifas con me feria"   You "trabaja" work (slang "chamba or jale") for your "sueldo" salary (slang "chivo," goat, or "raya," line). The kid's pocket money is his "domingo" or Sunday, traditionally given on that day as the preponderance of wages are pain weekly in Mexico - they don't stretch much further. When I left South Baja in 2002, the average weekly stipend was approximately 1000 pesos per week ($100 or £50). Many in the rural sector made less.

It won't surprise the eager credit card shoppers in the USA and the UK (the latter now has a credit card debt of more than one TRILLION! No doubt the US is several times that) to know the word for debt in

Mexico is "droga," the same as drug! Being out of the necessary can be "pelado," (peeled), "jorbado," (hunchbacked...don't you love this imagery?), or "brujo," a wizard...witch is a "bruja," and most Mexicans believe in sorcery, you'd better believe it, notwithstanding their protestations and denials! "Quinta" is another slang name for small change and to be "en la quinta" indicated total financial ruin, like being in the poorhouse.

Heard at the Border, the "Frontera."

The huge barrios (slums) of Los Angeles and Tijuana are the crucible from which much of Mexican border slang was formed, reformed and constantly added-to. Much finds its way south and that from the mainstream of Mexican culture is added to that of the border. The "Chicanos" living in California, etc., almost seem to have created their own "pidgin Spanish" as their limited vocabulary contains both bastardized US English and that of the Queen.

"Pachucos" Mexicans living in L.A., also known as "Cholos" or street urchins. The term becomes derogatory south of the border as Cholos take on an unsavory reputation. Heard in the prisons and on the streets of all the US border areas is the ubiquitous "Ese," (that) used to address someone (usually of "the blood") The English "watch" has been Latinized to "huatch" pronounced almost the same. "Ahi te huacho" is to give attention or used as a "see ya later" type of goodbye.

"Quiubo?" Howya going? Not a word, but a slurred version of "Que hubo?"

"Biklas," or "Bicis" derived from English for the same conveyances: bicycles or scooters. A cute one is "los beibidols" from the English "baby dolls" of course. Bluffing at cards is "blofeur," like "bluffear"

The spare Spanish "nada," mentioned herein, gets embellished in several ways, one being "nariz boleada" a nonsense meaning "buffed nose." The humorous hodgepodge of signs along the border such as "Se fixen flats" we repair punctures, or "meseras" (waitresses) who call for "crema de whip." And one unforgettable sign outside a café near the Texas border, "Fright cheeken!"

Sauce for the Goose ain't Sauce for McDonalds

Mexican law has occasionally got into the act where poaching foreign sayings is concerned. A friend began a fast-food restaurant in Mexico City in 1971 and was told he could not use the combination word "Gordoburgers," (fat burgers) but must use "Gordohamburguesas!" not half the cachet. As the Mexican word for hamburger (hamburguesa) is just a phonetically altered Americanism (Germanism?) and not a Spanish word, he found this mystifying. But the licensing authority wouldn't budge, not even with a "mordida" (bite, bribe).

In 2006, we have McDonald's everywhere saying what ever the hell a multi-trillion-dollar company wants to say: they even put up the hideous golden arch sign right next to a Colonial Church in Puebla's historic plaza! "Que gacho!"…"Que barbaridad!!"

The author hopes you have enjoyed glancing through this handbook of Mexican modismos and you will now – carefully – try some of the milder words or expressions on your Mexican friends. Mexicans love to laugh with you if you give them the opportunity, and attempting their very own street talk is guaranteed to impress and amuse them: remember, if you fall by the wayside using the slang in this modest book…don't kill the messenger!!

Robert Challen de Mercer.

Printed in the United States
135095LV00001B/90/A